CUSTOMER SERVICE
NEW RULES

Customer Service New Rules

Increase Your Profits by Providing
Exceptional Customer Service with
New Platinum Rules

Sophia Brooks

Library of Congress Control Number: 2009900976
ISBN: Hardcover   978-1-4415-0890-4
                           Softcover   978-1-4415-0889-8

To order additional copies of this book, contact:
Xlibris Corporation
1-888-795-4274
www.Xlibris.com
Orders@Xlibris.com
57712

Businesses that can benefit from this book:

- Restaurants
- Gift Shops
- Department Stores
- Grocery Stores
- Corporate Offices
- Professional Buildings
- Attorney Offices
- Medical Buildings
- Hospitals
- Fast Food Restaurants
- Movie Theaters
- DMV
- Manufacturing Facilities
- Construction Companies
- Government Facilities
- City Offices
- Engineering Firms
- Any Organization that has customer intervention face to face or on the phone . . . .

Contents

There are risks and costs to a program of action.
But they are far less than the long-range
risks and costs of comfortable inaction.

—John F. Kennedy

Preface

Exceptional customer service is a business issue and businesses the world over are taking a closer look at how they address it. More than this, customer service is a strategy on the annual goal chart, a part of employee performance reviews, a focus group topic, and number one on the satisfaction survey.

Providing *exceptional customer service* can be the survival key for your business.

This book, *Customer Service New Rules*, will help you and your organization deliver exceptional customer service, benefiting your frontline employees right away and guaranteeing the success and growth of your company in the long run. The governing board, senior-level executives, the management team players must all apply these new platinum rules to improve your company's customer service delivery and stay in business.

If you have been with an organization for many years, handling every type of customer service issue, or even if you are new to the customer service business, this information will help you maintain the momentum you need to grow your business.

Acknowledgments

Special heartfelt thanks to my husband and family for giving me the time and encouragement to write.

My appreciation also to the team at Global Learning Partners, Inc.

Customer Service
New Rules

Exceptional Customer Service New Rules You "Must Do's":

1. **Must hire people who have a service attitude.**

   Hire the attitude and train the skill. Hire people who enjoy serving others.

2. **Must never let an untrained employee have customer contact.**

   Cannot say this any other way. Untrained employees will lose you customers and money.

3. **Must make the customer's time with you an experience.**

   Each experience with the customer must be a positive customer experience (PCE).

4. **Must regularly inform all your employees about what's going on in your company.**

   It is very annoying and frustrating for your customers to ask a service agent of your company—a question and the response is "I don't know" It is your business to know.

5. **Must make every decision with the customer in mind.**

   Include the customer into your decision-making process. How will this decision affect my customer?

6. **Must make the customers an agenda item at every team meeting.**

   Never forget the reason you are having the meeting in the first place. Everything we do within the company is about the core "our customers."

7. **Must empower your employees to do the right thing.**

Train, train, train your employees.

8. **Must install continuous improvement initiatives.**

Include customer service as part of the company's performance appraisal process. Within the process, ask employees to write a customer service improvement goal. Do not forget to write a customer service goal for yourself.

9. **Must create an atmosphere of excellence.**

Let it be known that everything you and your employees do has to be the best, and you will not accept less. Pay attention to the smallest details.

10. **Must continually surprise the customer, do the unexpected.**

Many customers will no longer accept poor service, they will not continue to do business with you. You can increase your bottom line quickly by training employees to do the unexpected.

11. **"I repeat"—Must never let an untrained employee have customer contact.**

New Platinum Rule 1

Know the Business of Exceptional Customer Service

In the hospital, you call them patients.
At a luxury hotel, you call them guests.
On an airplane, you call them passengers.

Bottom line, they are your *customers*.
They are your *bottom line*.

Keeping their business depends on
how well you treat them.

The Business of Exceptional Customer Service

True customer service is bigger than your interaction with your various patrons, regardless of whether you are interacting over the telephone or in person, using e-mail, brochures, or press releases. At the same time, customer service is similar to a game of tennis. Those who fail to master the basics of serving well tend to lose more often than they win. The business of exceptional customer service starts with understanding and managing basic skills.

Service is the set of behaviors that employees undertake during an interaction with a customer. That interaction can be face-to-face, over the telephone, via e-mail, and other electronic communications. It must be focused on creating customer loyalty through customer satisfaction. If you are satisfying your customers, they are an extension of your sales and referral team. Keep up the great work. If you have loyal customers, you can increase your prices, relocate, change your product line, and they will continue to do business with you.

To create customer loyalty, employees must act as ambassadors for your business. You must develop ambassadors by

- hiring the right people,
- retaining talented people,
- living your positive culture,
- training your employees,
- making teamwork *work*,
- providing solutions not excuses, and
- celebrating often.

There are two main types of customers—internal and external customers—for whom you need to be working.

Internal customers are people you interact with on a regular basis. They come from other departments within the organization. They might be involved in human resources, payroll management, or department managers. Your internal customer wants to be treated with respect, courtesy, kindness, displaying a sense of urgency, and absolute accuracy.

External customers are individuals and organizations that make use of your products and services. Whether your organization manufactures double widgets or sells computers, it is critical to manage the buying experience of every customer. Your external customer wants to be treated with respect, courtesy, kindness, displaying a sense of urgency, and absolute accuracy. External customers want to be seen as individuals not a number.

Exceptional customer service depends on the type of product or services you and your organization offer to the public. Whether you are an independent consultant, a local bank, or a manager at the hospital, the foundation of exceptional customer service is *positive customer experience (PCE)*.

To create a PCE each and every time you engage with a customer, first, *never say no to a customer*. Yes, there will be times when *no* is the appropriate answer. I repeat, however, you do not want to say *no* right away. Customers do not want to hear it. Exhaust all options before saying *no*. Providing exceptional customer service means establishing *a set of behaviors that employees undertake during the customer* **interaction** *that promote PCE*.

The work environment for internal customers must be conducive to delivering exceptional customer service. Internal customers need to be held accountable (not responsible) for delivering PCEs. They must also be rewarded frequently when they are successful.

Each internal customer must believe and practice the philosophy that *"my job is to make your job easier."* If employees believe this and if they also believe that, their job is to make your customer's life easier; internal customer service will improve greatly, leading to an improvement in service to external customers.

Satisfied employees are more likely to be efficient, organized, and responsible members of your business. They are more likely to demonstrate respect, courtesy, kindness, and helpfulness toward your external customers.

—

Therefore, New Platinum Rule 1: The business of exceptional customer service includes never saying no to your customers during the first few minutes of the interaction. Also, employees buying into the belief that my job is to make your job easier.

External customers want to know what you can do for them, not what you cannot do for them. The customer comes to your business to get their needs met. Saying no to any of their requests means you are not doing your job.

Consider for a moment the number of times service providers actually say no to a customer. Exceptional service means putting a stop to this. The customers comes into the store wanting to buy a blue shirt; you have no blue shirts—expand the options for the customers, help them to see that a gray shirt is much better than a blue shirt. In many situations, you will need to educate the customer by expanding options to buy, buy, buy versus bye, bye, bye. Look at figure 1:1.

Figure 1:1.

Question from a customer	Average response	Saying no means	Exceptional response
Do you have this shirt in blue?	No, we don't	When we say no right away, the customer may leave without making a purchase. You will lose money.	Let me check our stock. We have yellow, white, and gray in that particular shirt. The white and gray can be used with a wide range of colors.
Do you have Acer computers on sale?	No, we don't	When we say no right away, the customer may leave without making a purchase. You will lose money.	Dell computers are on sale this week. Tell me what you are looking for in a computer, and perhaps we can save you some money today.

It is easy to say no—saying no allows us to be lazy. When you are in business to earn money, saying no to the customer is a strong indicator you do not want their money.

Saying no to a customer takes on different shapes. We say no every day without using the word "no." Here are a few "no sayers" without saying no—are any of these a part of your business?

Figure 1:2

Saying no without using the word "no"	Translation	What can you say?
We are closed.	You can't come in.	Make a decision now that you want your business to be profitable. And part of the platinum rule 1 says, "Never say no." Give me a call 951-549-1800 if you need help with creating standard *yes* responses for your customers.
We don't accept checks.	We don't want your money.	
We don't do that.	We don't want your business.	

Six steps are involved in the provision of exceptional customer service, and they are requirements *for all businesses*.

Step 1: Listen to what your customers want and need.

You are in business to meet the needs of your customers. The only way to know their needs is to listen. Listen with interest.

Step 2: Supply your finest service and ensure that it is provided on time.

If you promise to deliver a product or service at a certain time, ensure you meet your obligations. If, due to circumstances outside of your control, delivery is delayed, be honest with your customer and inform them of the situation. Offer compensation for their inconvenience. Compensation may look different based on the type of business. Work to alleviate the problem. Continuous improvement is critical for exceptional consumer service.

Step 3: Keep up with technology.

Strive to improve your services with technology that makes it easy for customers to use your products and services. Using technology may allow you to offer more to your customers and thus keeps them happy. Technology is the future, but humans supply the appreciation element.

Step 4: Offer a guarantee.

This is an important ingredient of exceptional customer service. When a *customer is 100 percent happy with* your service and products, they are your biggest and best asset. Referrals come from happy customers. If your customer is unhappy for any reason, fix the problem right away. If you trust and believe in your products and services, speak up and offer a guarantee. The guarantee will vary based on the industry; here are a few examples:

- One hundred percent satisfaction or get your money back
- A free car wash
- A coupon for your next visit
- A sixty-day money back
- A free dessert

Step 5: Provide prompt responses to all communications and inquiries.

Customers do not like to wait. You must respond to them within twenty-four hours or less. Technology can help with this, but e-mails do not send themselves. The longer you wait to respond to an inquiry or request, the greater the chance your customer will move onto another provider.

Step 6: Manners matters.

Whether interactions involve asking for a quote or dealing with a complaint, treat your customer very well. When customers complain, thank them for bringing the problem to your attention. Always be present, be polite, and be focused on making the customer happy.

Understanding the 13-1 survey

You can do everything right 99 percent of the time, but if your customer has a bad experience, the bad experience is what they will remember. For every thirteen good experiences your customer has with your business, they may tell one person about you. On the other hand, if the customer has a bad experience, they will tell thirteen people about it if the problem goes uncorrected.

A customer is the most important visitor on our premises.
He or she is not dependent on us—we are dependent on him or her.

Four Points to Remember:

1. PCE is an acronym for positive customer experience. Each interaction with the customer is extremely important. We don't get a second chance.

2. Service is manifested as a set of behaviors that employees undertake while interacting with customers.

3. Service must be focused on treating customers with respect, courtesy, kindness, displaying a sense of urgency and absolute accuracy.

4. Truly loyal customers will let you increase your prices, relocate, and change your product line; they will continue to do business with you.

New Platinum Rule 2

Know Your Customer's Name

See someone without a smile?
Give them one of yours.

Know Your Customer's Name

Businesses that deliver a positive customer experience (PCE) each time understand the benefits of using the name of their customer during interactions. Most of us have experienced an embarrassing moment of forgetting someone's name. It can be awkward and uncomfortable.

For businesses, it is important to use the customer's name during the interaction—sincerely, say the customer's name.

In addition, everyone in the business must *smile*. We all want to go where people are happy to service us, and they know our name. When possible, use the customer's name. It is good business to let your customer know you remember them.

Consider for a moment the customer loyalty and customer satisfaction levels of your company. Seven years ago, I moved into a small community free of congestion and traffic. I selected Smith's Dry Cleaners; they were located in a strip center near my home, and the prices were reasonable. As the community grew, the strip center became jam-packed with businesses, people, and cars.

Several other dry cleaners moved into the community. The new dry cleaners were closer to my home. I tried the new dry cleaners and was extremely dissatisfied with their service. My items were not ready when promised. Employees were unfriendly. I quickly returned to Smith's Dry Cleaners where everyone knew my name, and the service was great.

The employees at Smith's Dry Cleaners not only provide me with great service and smiles as I enter the door, they use my name each time, and they invite me back each time. Their total customer service package is very simple yet very effective. As I leave the dry cleaners, the employee says to me, "It was good to see you today, Mrs. Brooks, I'll see you next time." By saying this to me as I head out of their door, they assure there is a next time.

To get to know your customer, it is also important to regularly ask for feedback after interaction. Ask your customers about the service they received. Are they happy with it? Make the question specific. Say, "On a scale of 1 to 10, how would we rate the service you received today?" If the customer rates the service 5.5, say, "Thank you so much for the feedback. We strive for tens. Any suggestions on what we can do to improve our rating?"

Do not say, "How was our service today?" The customer can find an easy out by saying, "Oh, the service was *fine*."

Teach everyone in the organization to use the customer's name. In today's fast-paced environments where unfriendly and discourteous service is commonplace, this will make a huge difference. Try it—your customers will love it and this will have a strong impact on future business. "Everyone wants to go where someone knows their name."

When using the customer's name, follow this simple formula "I VALUE U"

I	Introduce your self, this can be simple "good morning"
V	Vibrant (be lively, energetic and excited the customer is doing business with you
A	Always make eye contact
L	Listen to the customer
U	Understand the customer's needs, and repeat back what you heard
E	Extend a "Thank You" for doing business with us
U	Use the customer's name

During our field research, results indicated employees saying thank you because it is part of the script. The script was ineffective. It sounds like this

"Thank you—NEXT CUSTOMER," no sincere kindness in their voice. Being courteous and sincere are critical parts of the I VALUE U formula. Use these words with enthusiasm

- Please
- Thank You
- May I help you
- Is there anything else I can do for you today? It is critical to ask this question of all customers before they leave. This is a small part of up-selling and this is your last time to make a lasting impression on the customer.

Customer satisfaction creates customer loyalty. Positive Customer Experience (PCE) is directly related to the interaction between the employee and the customer.

In today's competitive market providing world-class service is the key to increasing your profits. And it is the simple yet powerful attention to details that will keep your customers coming back.

Employees must meet and exceed customers' expectations.

I recommend that you evaluate your organization's "service", This is different from asking your customer to evaluate their interaction with your business. This is asking employees to evaluate various departments within the organization.

Visit *www.glpcustomerservice*.com to request information on how to conduct effective customer service surveys.

When the customer comes first, the customer will last.

—Robert Half

Four Points to Remember:

1. Everyone in the business must *smile*. In today's fast-paced environment, unfriendly and discourteous service is commonplace. A smile will make a huge difference.

2. Everyone in the business must be courteous. This means they should be sincere and use certain words and phrases with enthusiasm ("Please," "Thank you," "May I help you?").

3. Everyone in the business must ask for feedback from the customer. It is important to end customer interaction with two questions: "Is there anything else I can do for you?" and "How would you rate the service you received today?" It is your last chance to ensure that you make a positive impression on the customer.

4. Everyone in the business is responsible for inviting the customer to come back. A direct invitation is quite simply the best way to ensure that the customer will come back.

5. Bonus—*smile*; a smile is the same in every language.

New Platinum Rule 3

Being Exceptional

Your first job is to build a relationship with your customer. This comes before you introduce your product and services. Make a positive impression from the very first.

Know How to "Be Exceptional"

A culture of exceptional customer service is not a quick fix. It will take a strong training initiative, changes in policies and practices, systems for holding people accountable, effective hiring practices, and procedures for firing people who do not meet expectations.

Here are ten steps your business can implement to get started with creating a culture of "being exceptional." Each department must be in alignment with these steps for the process to work.

Step 1: Establish the "service attitude"

The organization's mission, vision, and core values must address and communicate an attitude of service. This is much more than words on the wall. The organization must walk, talk, and live a positive attitude to service. A service attitude is one that embraces diversity.

Step 2: Establish a "service focus"

Install customer sensitive language within policies, procedures, and job descriptions. Consider language to describe "employees" as a reflection of their value and importance to the business success. Employees must be ambassadors for your business they are the front line. Some business use partners, associates, or team members versus saying employees.

Step 3: Establish a habit of paying attention to the smallest of details

It's the little things that make a big difference in the exceptional customer service experience. Respond to customers versus reacting to customers.

Step 4: Establish leadership at all levels

Hold employees accountable for delivering exceptional service, regardless of title or position. Create leaders at all levels within the organization.

Provide frequent opportunities for executives to perform frontline duties. Set standards and measure performance.

Step 5: Establish a process for hiring and keep quality employees

Improve recruiting and selection processes. Develop innovative strategies for hiring only the best people for exceptional service. Hire customer-sensitive people, train them carefully and extensively.

Step 6: Establish a system where your employees replace "I'm sorry" with "I apologize"

We have all heard customer service representatives say "I'm sorry." Often, we want to reply with "yes, you are sorry!" We know the customer service representative is not really sorry. I recommend that you "kick it up a notch" if you want to stand out. Say, "I apologize, I know I can help!" Stand back and watch this work. Keep in mind that positive body language and an attitude of helpfulness are important too. Be a professional, not a sorry customer service agent.

Step 7: Establish a rule for active listening not excessive talking

Yes, you have heard the same question three hundred times. Yes, you know the answer, but you must let the customer talk. Do not interrupt; do not finish the customer sentences.

Step 8: Establish a practice of underpromising and overdelivering

First and foremost, do not promise the customer something you cannot deliver. Be specific as to what you can do. Always summarize what you plan to do for the customer. Put yourself in the customer's shoes.

Step 9: Establish a system to report and eliminate nuisances

Eliminate anything in the customer's environment that is negative. Such as doors that are difficult to open or close. When interacting with the customer, make a conscious effort to minimize the use of negative words and phrases; always start with a positive statement when interacting with customers.

Step 10: Establish a PCE team

The purpose of the team is to install exceptional customer service practices, policies and internal and external satisfaction surveys. This will consist of a cross section of employees from various departments.

Four Points to Remember:

1. Being exceptional means incredible service provided by friendly and knowledgeable employees.

2. Being exceptional means having a service attitude—do not let customers feel invisible. Acknowledge the customer's presence. Look at the customer and say "thank you for coming in today." When customers are in line waiting to be served, make eye contact with the next person in line, smile, and nod your head. Let the customer know in a nonverbal way they are not invisible.

3. Being exceptional means creating a culture where everyone is focused on providing exceptional service. Departmental goals are in alignment with exceptional customer service.

4. Being exceptional means paying attention to the smallest details. From the point of service, pay attention to the total interaction with the customer.

New Platinum Rule 4

Communicating Like an Ambassador

> There is only one boss—the customer. And he can fire anybody in the company from the chairman on down, simply by spending his money somewhere else.
>
> —Sam Walton

Communicating Like an Ambassador

ambassador

am*bas"sa*dor\, embassador \em*bas"sa*dor\, n.]

1. The highest ranking diplomat who represents their country. Accredited to a foreign sovereign or government, to serve as the official representative of their country.
2. An official messenger and representative.

An ambassador has a mission and strong purpose. The ambassador must be able to converse effectively to many. In customer service, you must be able to converse effectively to many.

Let's dissect communication and create a traditional model.

Figure 1:3

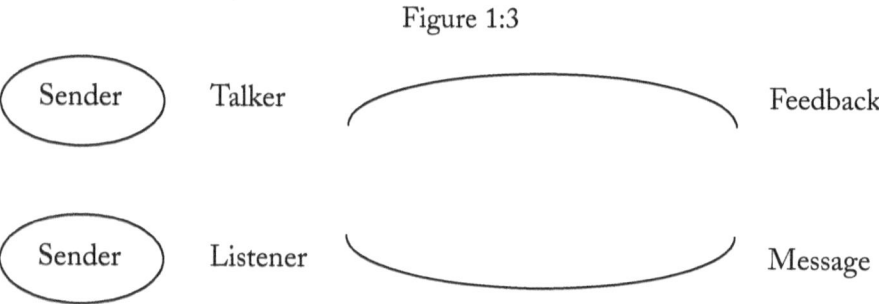

Sender   Talker   Feedback

Sender   Listener   Message

Put these together with a model of communicating such as face-to-face or over the telephone. And we have a communication model that can be very complex.

Figure 1:4

The Communication Model

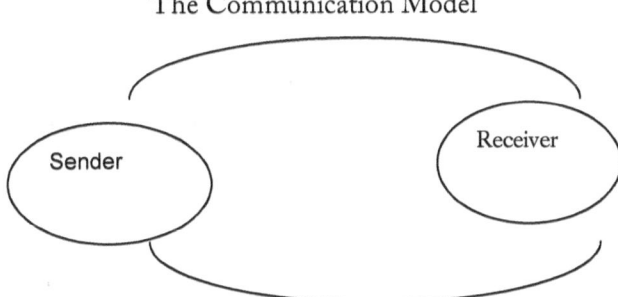

Effective communication is a catalyst for exceptional customer service.

- Everything we do communicates something.
- Whenever contact is made with a customer, communication occurs.
- Meanings are communicated through people, not through words.
- Although all communications are received, 70 percent to 90 percent are screened out or changed by the receiver (listener) of the message.

Attitude, appearance, positive posture, tone of voice, and word choices are part of the communication model. All of the above can be positive in the model or negative in the model.

To provide exceptional customer service, I recommend being positive in all of the above. Here is how attitude, appearance, positive posture, tone of voice, and word choices fit into the model.

Figure 1:4

Attitude

Customer service is 80 percent attitude and 20 percent technique.

Attitude is a key element of communicating with internal and external customers. Customers expect to interact with positive upbeat people.

At the end of the day, attitude has the potential to make a boring job fun and a fun job boring. We are in control of our attitude. Practice creating a positive inner-dialog daily. An inner dialog is our self-talk. It is what we tell ourselves about an event. As an example, your day started with a telephone call from an irate customer. The second customer you interacted with was upset with a previous purchase and blames you. Your boss (who is your internal customer) wants to meet with you regarding a missed deadline. So your inner dialog (self-talk) may become filled with "Oh my, what's going to happen next? If one more thing goes wrong, I am going to scream."

Instead of screaming, create a positive inner dialog about the events of the day. Practice saying something like this: "this day is filled with challenges; I am skilled, confident, and prepared to handle the challenges of the day. I will not allow the events of the day to affect my interaction with my next customer."

Appearance

Look at your appearance; is it appropriate for your position with the organization? Are you following the organization dress code? The customer sees you as the company. It does not matter if you are the receptionist, field representative, or the hospital operator, you are the organization. Dress professionally for the position you hold within the organization. It will infuse motivation into your day.

Positive Posture

A professional image starts with your posture and makes a lasting impression on your customers. Stand up straight and sit up straight; this will improve your internal mood.

Tone of Voice

Our tone of voice and inflections communicates our attitude to the customer. The customer can surmise from our tone of voice if we are hurried, confident, angry, annoyed, and much more.

A strong part of delivering exceptional customer service involves using a professional and sincere tone of voice.

Your voice has a
speed
direction
rhythm
pitch
smoothness
harmony
emphasis
tempo

Word Choices

When delivering exceptional customer service, be aware of your word choices. As an example, in a hospital environment, the patient (your customer) asks for something for pain. The next pain medication for the patient (your customer) is scheduled to be administered in one hour. The nurse could easily say, "I'm sorry, I can't give you anything for pain for another hour."

I recommend that the nurse use the patient's name and say, "Yes, Mr. Brooks, I will bring your next dosage for pain in at 6:00 p.m., which is your next schedule time. Let me adjust your pillow, would you like some water?"

Saying "I'm sorry" is a poor choice of words. No customer wants to hear about what they cannot have. Tell the customer in a positive way what you can do, not what you *cannot* do. I call this reframing to deliver exceptional customer service.

In an attempt to impress, we may use too many technical terms and acronyms. Do not overwhelm your customers with too much information. Keep it simple.

When interacting with customers, work diligently to give a positive before the negative. When delivering exceptional customer service, there are some things we never, never say to customers:

This New Platinum Rule 4: Communicating like an ambassador includes this big never

It's imperative in communicating with the customer to avoid saying, "I don't know." Customers want you to know.

Figure 1:5

Things to avoid saying to a customer	Reframed to say
Average response	Exceptional response
I don't know.	Let me find out for you.
That's not my department.	John is very familiar with that area and knows the ins and outs—let me get John to help you right now.
I'm new.	One moment please, I will . . .
I'm busy with another customer.	I appreciate your patience; thank you so much. I will be with you in a few minutes.

Asking Questions

There is magic in asking customers the right questions, asking questions that will empower them (not you). This skill is not taught in school. For more information on *The Skillful Question*, send your request via e-mail to customerservice@glpinc.com.

Ineffective questions	Effective questions
Is there anything else?	What else can I help you with today?
Is this all?	What else can I get for you today?

Four Points to Remember:

1. Customer service is 80 percent attitude and 20 percent technique. It is very important to the success of a company that every single employee is focused on maintaining a positive attitude.

2. Never say "I don't know" or "no" to a customer. If they ask you a question to which you do not know the answer, first say what you know, such as "I know that *x* will be able to answer that" or "I know we have *y* on sale today." You must always find a way around saying "no." If a customer asks for something that you cannot do, start by saying what you can do.

3. Asking effective questions improves the communication process. Empower your customer so that they ask for the help they need; help them to help you believe in exceptional service.

4. Having a positive posture plays a role in effective communication. So long as you are positive and friendly, you will have customers who are loyal to you and your company.

New Platinum Rule 5

Burn Bright without Burning Out

Spend your energy
searching for solutions.
Do not waste it on excuses.

Burning Bright without Burning Out

It is important to manage your stress when working with customers. If constant stress has you feeling physically, mentally, and emotionally exhausted, you may be suffering from burnout. Day-to-day interaction with customers may seem insurmountable. It may be difficult to gather up the energy to deliver exceptional customer service all the time. This is why you need to be active in preventing burnout.

Recognizing Burnout

Burnout is a state of emotional and physical exhaustion caused by excessive and prolonged stress. It can occur when you feel overwhelmed and unable to meet constant demands. Burnout reduces your productivity and zaps your energy, leaving you feeling increasingly hopeless, powerless, cynical, and resentful.

All these feelings will hamper your ability to deliver exceptional customer service. The unhappiness can even threaten your job, your relationships, and your health.

Signs and Symptoms of Burnout

The signs of burnout tend to manifest themselves mentally as well as physically. They can include:

- Emotional exhaustion
- Slumped shoulders
- Irritability
- Lazy walk
- Detachment
- Poor posture
- Frustration
- Despair
- Cynicism

If you are feeling burned out, you might find yourself always snapping at customers or making snide remarks about them. You might feel depressed, on the other hand, and want to sleep all the time. You might simply feel "too tired" to work.

Job Burnout

Burnout is common in the workplace, but there is a difference between a bad workday and job burnout. Most of us have days when we feel bored, overloaded, or unappreciated.

Workplace burnout is not the same as workplace stress. When you are stressed, you care too much. When you are burned out, you do not see any hope of improvement.

Causes of Job Burnout

While some careers have higher rates of burnout, the problem exists for workers in every occupation. Those most at risk are employees who feel underpaid, underappreciated, or overcriticized for matters beyond their control. Customer service professionals who spend their work lives attending to the needs of others can be particularly susceptible.

Causes of job burnout include:

- Setting unrealistic goals for yourself or having them imposed upon you
- Being expected to be too many things to too many people
- Working under rules that seem unreasonably
- Doing work that frequently causes you to violate your personal values
- Boredom from doing work that never changes or doesn't challenge you
- Feeling trapped for economic reasons by a job that fits any of the scenarios above

Preventing Job Burnout

Clarify your job description. Ask your supervisor for an updated description of your job duties and responsibilities. Or use the existing job description to create new job description for your position. You may then be able to point out that some of the things you are expected to do are not part of your job description. This approach can gain you a little leverage by showing that you've been working outside and above the parameters of your job.

If you are truly unhappy in your position, request a transfer within the organization. Talk to your supervisor about feeling the need to change and grow in different professional areas.

You may not like this option, but it can be very powerful. Ask for new or additional duties or projects. If you've been doing the exact same work for a long time, ask to try something new: a different grade level, a different sales territory, a different machine, a different department.

Take time off. If burnout seems inevitable, take a complete break from work. Go on a vacation to relax, no high-pressure vacation, a relaxing vacation—perhaps a local trip.

Preventing Burnout:

- Educate yourself
- Join a support group
- Know your limits
- Accept your feelings
- Confide in someone you trust
- Manage your time
- Manage your stress
- Connect with a cause or a community group
- Practice health and wellness

You should teach yourself and your employees to relax and take personal time on a regular basis, whether it is ten minutes at lunchtime or an hour after work, sitting at home. The key to preventing burnout is recognizing your limits and understanding that part of ensuring your best performance involves rewarding yourself for doing a good job.

Four Points to Remember:

1. Learn to recognize the signs and symptoms of burnout. Burnout can be a major problem for even the best of companies if it goes undetected and unaddressed.

2. Burnout can leave even the best of customer service providers depressed and deflated. The most common symptoms include lack of energy, lack of motivation, mood swings, exhaustion, and detachment.

3. The most common causes of job burnout include having unrealistic goals, overwork, unreasonable work conditions, and boredom.

4. The best way to prevent burnout is to educate yourself and your employees, take time to relax and reward yourself for positive customer service performance, and learn to accept your own (and your employees' limitations).

New Platinum Rule 6

Is the Customer Always Right?

> You can please some of the people all of the time, you can please all of the people some of the time, but you can't please all of the people all of the time.
>
> —John Lydgate

Is the Customer Always Right?

To provide exceptional customer service, you have to be prepared to support both your employees and your customers. You have to recognize the importance of your customers and your employees, creating an environment in which they can work together effectively.

If the customer is always right, does that mean the employees are wrong? No customer is right all of the time. If you adopt that practice, you will disenfranchise your employees.

Is the customer always right? No. However, I believe and practice that "there is always a right way to treat the customer."

Consider the story of a woman who truly disliked the service she received from South Shore Airlines. Despite disliking the company, the woman chose to fly with South Shore on a regular basis. Because she flew with the airline so frequently, and so often complains, she was known as the Pen Pal by the group of South Shore employees who handled the customer complaints. After virtually every flight, she wrote in with a complaint.

It seemed she disliked everything about the company—the fact that it didn't assign seats, that there was no first-class section, that there was no meal served in-flight. She even complained about the boarding procedure, the casual atmosphere, and the flashy uniforms of the flight attendants.

The last letter South Shore received from this disgruntled customer was sent on up to the desk of the company CEO. Reviewing the letter, it took the CEO all of sixty seconds to formulate a response, which went as follows:

"Dear Mrs. Crabtree, We will miss you. Good-bye."

Treat all customers and complaints seriously. If there is a customer issue, work diligently to resolve it.

The goal is to "keep customers." There are uncommon situations when you have to say, "Dear Mrs. Crabtree, We will miss you. Good-bye."

Avoiding the Us and Them Situation

In practice, if your customer is always right, your employees must always be wrong (at least in a dispute). This alienates your employees from your customers and could make the employees rather unhappy.

Mr. Brown is the man credited with turning Central Airlines around. To ensure that both customers and employees were happy with his company, Central Airlines, he went out of his way to argue that the "the customer is always right" really did not hold any weight.

In conflicts between employees and unreasonable customers, Mr. Brown would consistently side with his employees:

> When we run into customers that we can't reel back in, our loyalty is with our employees. They have to put up with this stuff every day. Just because you buy a ticket does not give you the right to abuse our employees . . . We run more than three million people through our books every month. One or two of those people are going to be unreasonable, demanding jerks. When it's a choice between supporting your employees, who work with you every day and make your product or service what it is, or some irate jerk who demands a free ticket to Paris because you ran out of peanuts, whose side are you going to be on? You can't treat your employees like ponds. You have to value them . . . If they think that you won't support them when a customer is out of line, even the smallest problem can cause resentment.

Put Your Trust in Your Employees

Trust the judgment of your employees when you are faced with unreasonable customers. Although you should always try to treat your customers with the utmost respect and dedication, if you don't distinguish between reasonable customers and unreasonable customers, you are going to leave a lot of disgruntled employees in your wake. It's as bad as, if not worse than, leaving disgruntled customers.

To provide exceptional customer service, you have to face the reality of abusive customers. At some point, you'll discover that abrasive and abusive customers are in the practice of demanding just about anything. If you allow that your customer is "always right," then they can behave as if they are right by definition, making your employees' job much harder. By treating your abrasive customers as if they are always right, you also establish an inappropriate reward system; the abusive people get treated as well, if not better than those who are nice and polite to your employees.

Firing Your Customers

Some customers are truly bad for business, and your customer service approach must recognize this too, if you want to provide exceptional service.

Smith's, an IT provider, told a story relevant to this about one of their service technicians and their experience with a customer. As the story goes, the technician arrived at a customer's site for a maintenance task. Upon arrival, the technician was treated very rudely by the customer and their staff. After completing their work and returning to the office, the service technician told their manager about their experience. The manager promptly contacted the company to explain their policy on acceptable and unacceptable treatment to their employees while performing their duties.

You may not feel as if exceptional customer service can ever involve firing a customer like this; but in reality, firing customers, when their attitude and behavior is disturbing for your employees, helps you to maintain a higher level of customer service overall. This is a uncommon practice, yet it does happen. Abusive treatment and behaviors from customers is unacceptable.

Seeing the Big Picture

Delivering exceptional customer service, if you put employees first, they will be happy at work and better equipped to provide the highest quality of customer service because:

- They care more about internal and external customers.
- They have more energy.
- They are happy, meaning they are more fun to talk to and interact with.
- They are more motivated.

This is the big picture as far as customer service goes. If you can keep these points in mind, you are well on your way to providing exceptional customer service and winning your bid to creating a loyal, dedicated customer base to support your business.

The customer is not always right;
There is "always" a right way to treat the customer.

—Sophia Brooks

Four Points to Remember:

1. Learn to trust and value your employees. Despite what most customer service experts tell you, *the customer is not always right.* However, there is *"always a right way to treat the customer."* Some customers will never be satisfied by what you do for them, and they will never be loyal to your company.

2. Support your employees so they can support your customers. By helping your employees (your internal customers), you facilitate positive customer experience (PCE) and help everyone in your organization reach their full potential.

3. Fire customers who undermine the value of your organization. Customers who make serious demands upon your time, energy, and resources, generally, are not worth the trouble. Let them go—politely, quietly, professionally, but let them go!

4. Recognize the big picture, the root cause of exceptional customer service. Give your employees the power to provide, and they will generally outperform.

Summary

Always have a customer service strategy. Reading this book, you have been exposed to the principle strategy for providing exceptional customer service, a strategy that is tested, tried, and proven as a means of providing exceptional customer service to a targeted audience.

Ensure that you and your team treat customers with respect, courtesy, kindness; display a sense of urgency and absolute accuracy. Be supportive of your customers, focused on accommodating their needs and providing the highest possible level of service by modifying your behavior and even your language to reflect a positive attitude at all times. Exceptional service is 80 percent attitude and 20 percent technique.

We explored how important it is to have a business culture of being exceptional. You know how to sell your company through your customer service, addressing the needs of your customers and providing them with the best possible benefits. Bring both your attitude and appearance in line with your company's values.

We are customer service experts. We can help you increase your profits with installing the platinum rules for exceptional customer service.

Global Learning Partners, Inc.
www.glpinc.com
951-549-1800

Further Resources

- *The Big Book of Customer Service Training Games*
  by Peggy Carlaw and Vasudha Kathleen Deming
  (Paperback—Oct. 1, 2006)

- *The Employee's Guide to Superior Customer Service*
  (DVD—Jan. 2, 2007)

- *Customer Service Crackpots*
  by Touch-Tone Terrorists and Junkyard Willie Prank Call Tapes
  (Audio CD—Mar. 18, 2002)

- *Customer Service Training 101: Quick and Easy Techniques That Get Great Results*
  by Renee Evenson
  (Paperback—Sep. 2, 2005)

- *Delivering Exceptional Customer Service*
  by Richard Mulvey
  (DVD—Oct. 29, 2007)

- *Super Service: Seven Keys to Delivering Great Customer Service . . . Even When You Don't Feel Like It! . . . Even When They Don't Deserve It!*
  by Jeff Gee and Val Gee
  (Paperback—Jul. 26, 1999)

Index